What

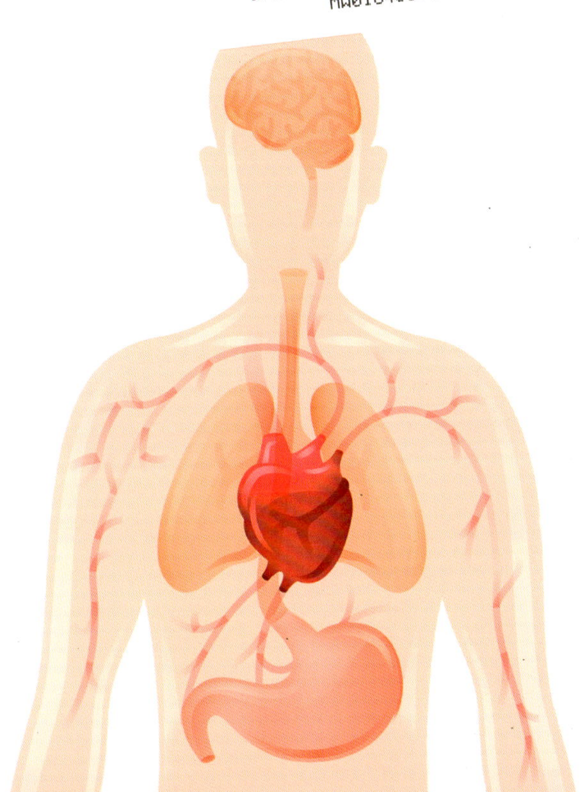

What is inside my head?

My brain is inside my head.

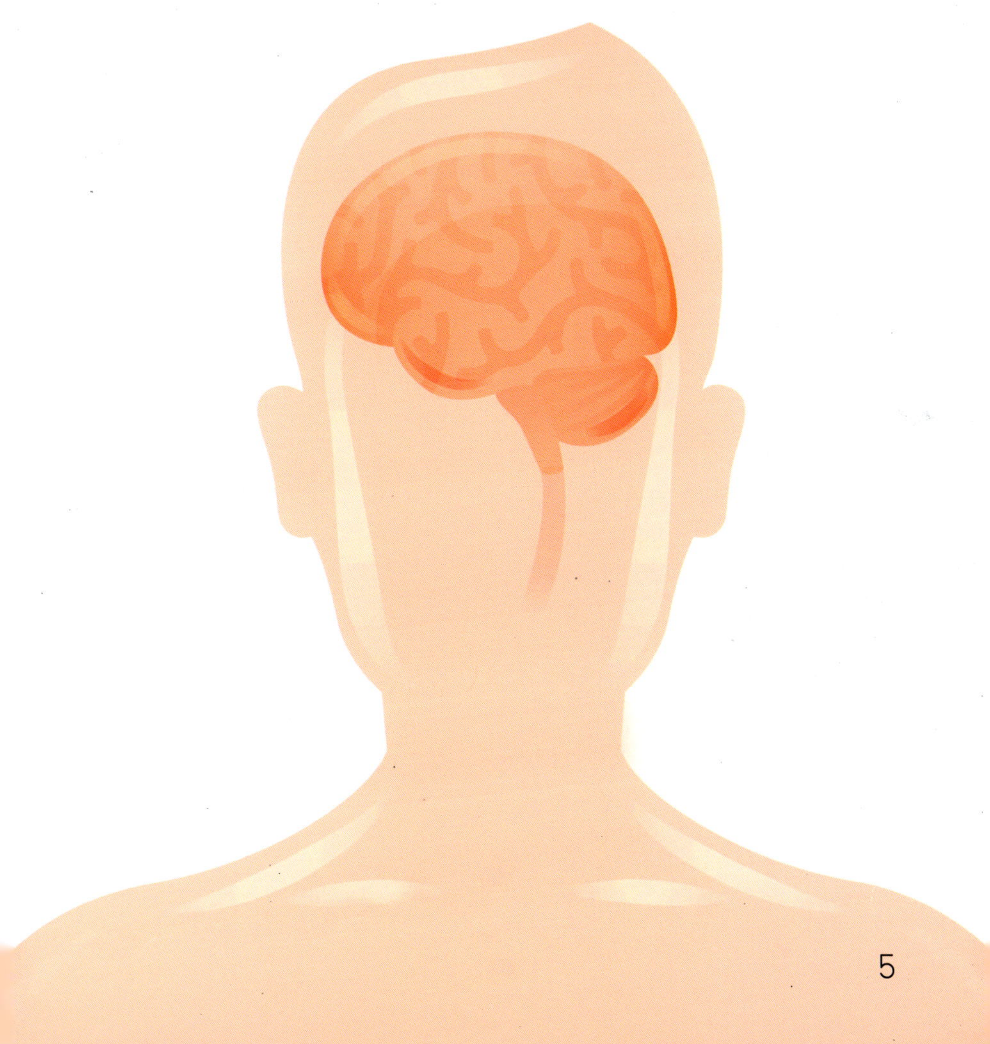

What is inside my belly?

My stomach is inside my belly.

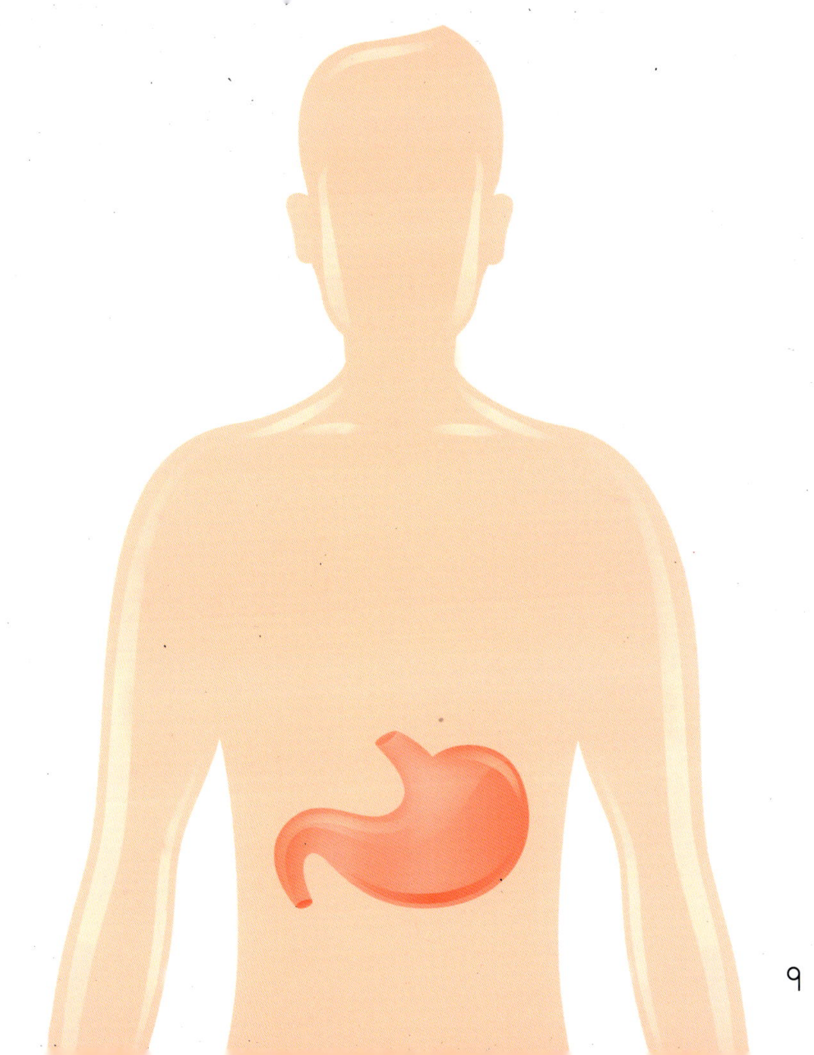

What is inside my chest?

My lungs are inside my chest.

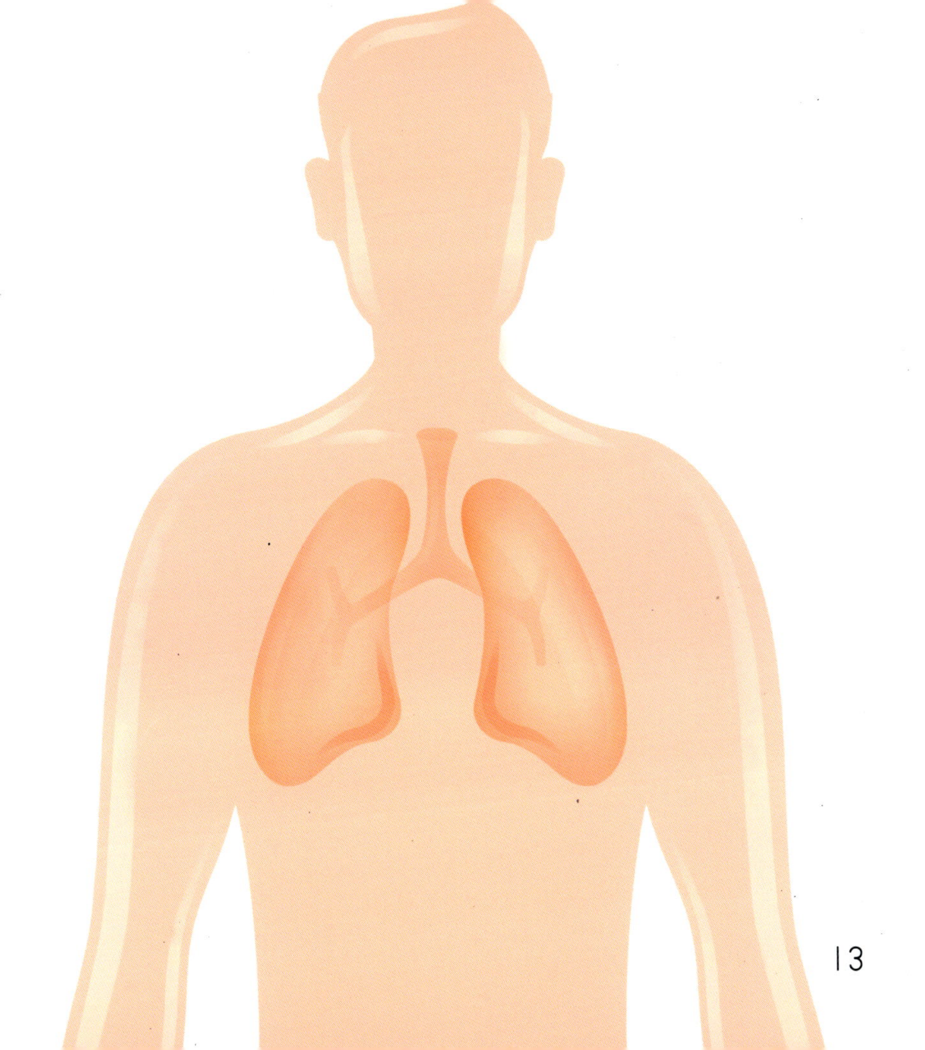

My heart is inside my chest, too.

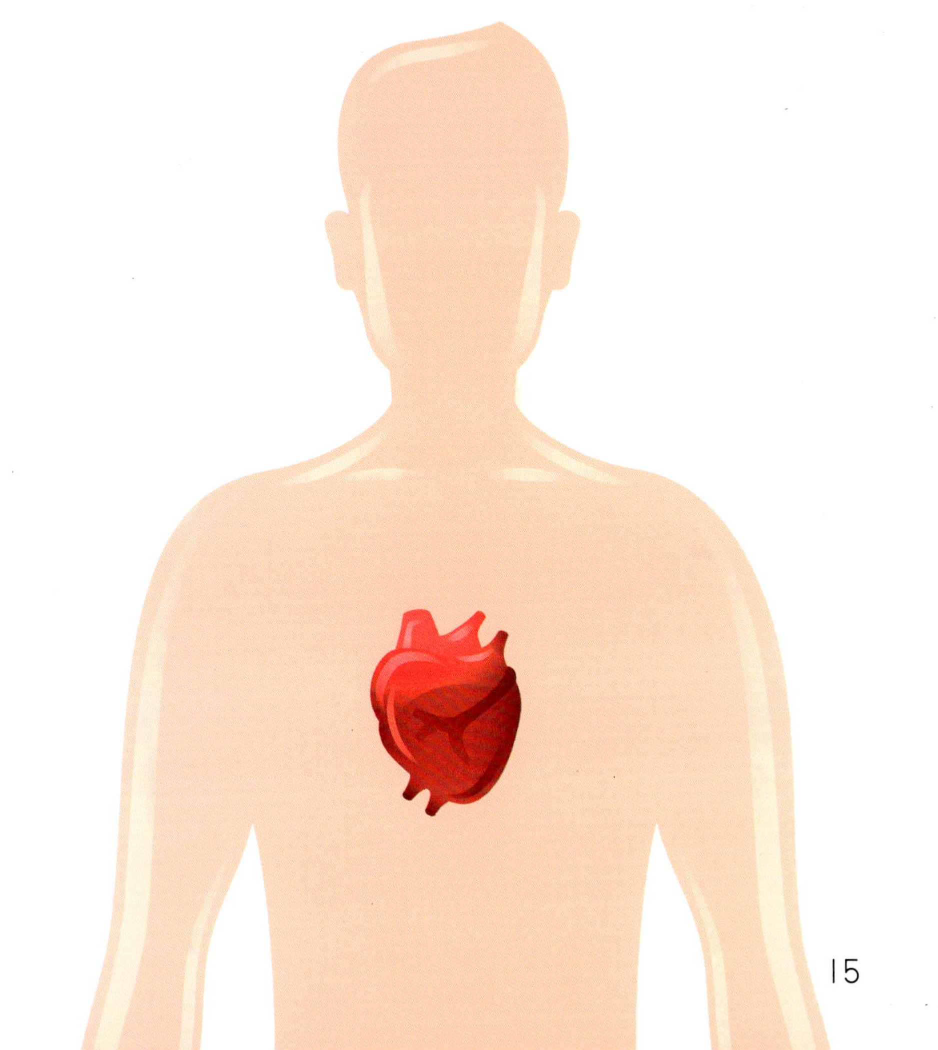

Look at what is inside me!

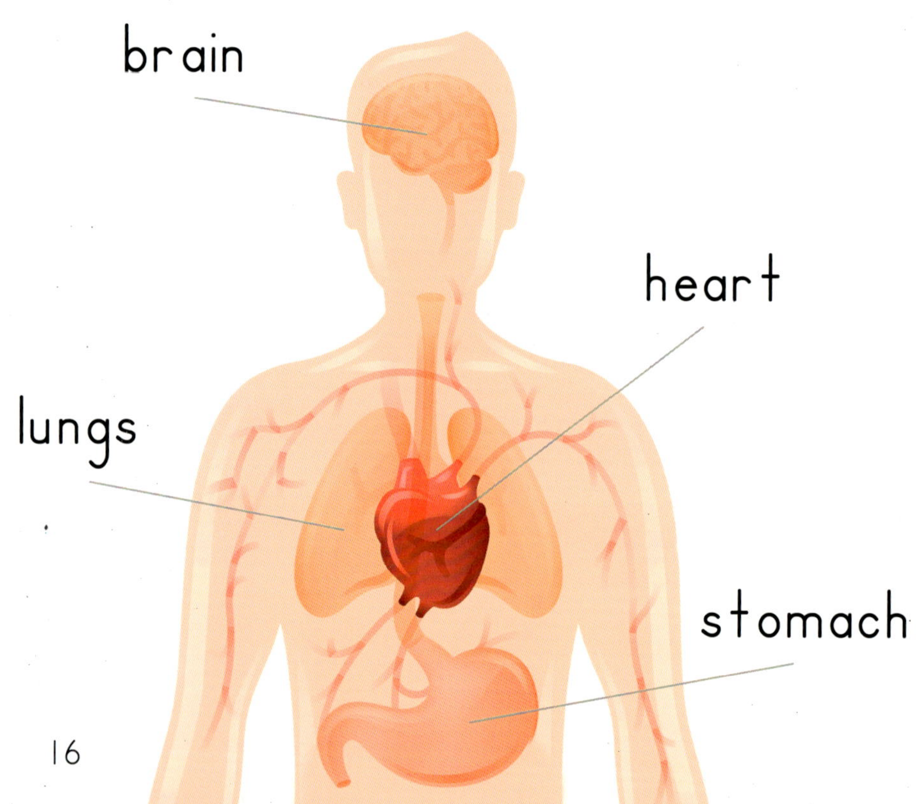